Formin

d on or before

THE EUROPEAN HUMANITIES RESEARCH CENTRE

UNIVERSITY OF OXFORD

Director: Martin McLaughlin
Fiat-Serena Professor of Italian Studies

The European Humanities Research Centre of the University of Oxford organizes a range of academic activities, including conferences and workshops, and publishes scholarly works under its own imprint, LEGENDA. Within Oxford, the EHRC bridges, at the research level, the main humanities faculties: Modern Languages, English, Modern History, Classics and Philosophy, Music and Theology. The Centre stimulates interdisciplinary research collaboration throughout these subject areas and provides an Oxford base for advanced researchers in the humanities.

The Centre's publishing programme focuses on making available the results of advanced research in medieval and modern languages and related interdisciplinary areas. An Editorial Board, whose members are drawn from across the British university system, covers the principal European languages. Titles currently include works on Arabic, Catalan, Chinese, English, French, German, Italian, Portuguese, Russian, Spanish, Greek and Yiddish literature. In addition, the EHRC co-publishes with the Society for French Studies, the Modern Humanities Research Association and the British Comparative Literature Association. The Centre also publishes a Special Lecture Series under the LEGENDA imprint, and a journal, *Oxford German Studies*.

Further information:
Kareni Bannister, Senior Publications Officer
European Humanities Research Centre
University of Oxford
76 Woodstock Road, Oxford OX2 6HP
enquiries@ehrc.ox.ac.uk
www.ehrc.ox.ac.uk

LEGENDA EDITORIAL BOARD

Chairman
Professor Martin McLaughlin, Magdalen College

Editorial Adviser
Professor Malcolm Bowie, Christ's College, Cambridge

Professor Ian Maclean, All Souls College (French)
Professor Marian Hobson Jeanneret, Queen Mary University of London (French)
Professor Ritchie Robertson, St John's College (German)
Professor Lesley Sharpe, University of Exeter (German)
Dr Diego Zancani, Balliol College (Italian)
Professor David Robey, University of Reading (Italian)
Dr Stephen Parkinson, Linacre College (Portuguese)
Professor Helder Macedo, King's College London (Portuguese)
Professor Gerald Smith, New College (Russian)
Professor David Shepherd, University of Sheffield (Russian)
Dr David Pattison, Magdalen College (Spanish)
Dr Alison Sinclair, Clare College, Cambridge (Spanish)
Professor Martin Maiden, Trinity College (Linguistics)
Professor Peter Matthews, St John's College, Cambridge (Linguistics)
Dr Elinor Shaffer, School of Advanced Study, London (Comparative Literature)
Professor Colin Davis, University of Warwick (Modern Literature, Film and Theory)

Senior Publications Officer
Kareni Bannister

Publications Officer
Dr Graham Nelson

LEGENDA

European Humanities Research Centre
Special Lecture Series

This series publishes a selection of public lectures in the Humanities given at the University of Oxford and was established to mark the 150th anniversary of the Taylor Institution.

Previously published in this series:

1. *Proust: Questions d'identité*
   by Julia Kristeva

2. *History Painting and Narrative*
   by Peter Brooks

3. *L'écriture testamentaire à la fin du Moyen Age: Identité, dispersion, trace*
   by Jacqueline Cerquiglini-Toulet

4. *Le partage de la parole*
   by Luce Irigaray

5. *A Self-Administered Poison: The System and Functions of Soviet Censorship*
   by Arlen Blyum

NEWCASTLE UNIVERSITY LIBRARY

203 31795 1

791437 GOD (Ber)

Brigitte Bardot in Jean-Luc Godard's 'Contempt' ('Le Mépris')
By permission of Canal+ Image UK Ltd

Forming Couples: Godard's *Contempt*

❖

Leo Bersani and Ulysse Dutoit

LEGENDA

European Humanities Research Centre
University of Oxford
Special Lecture Series 6
2003

Published by the
European Humanities Research Centre
of the University of Oxford
47 Wellington Square
Oxford OX1 2JF

LEGENDA is the publications imprint of the
European Humanities Research Centre

ISBN 1 904713 00 9
ISSN 1466–8165

First published 2003

All rights reserved. No part of this publication may be reproduced or disseminated or transmitted in any form or by any means, electronic, mechanical, photocopying, recording or otherwise, or stored in any retrieval system, or otherwise used in any manner whatsoever without the express permission of the copyright owner

British Library Cataloguing in Publication Data
A CIP catalogue record for this book is available from the British Library

© *Leo Bersani and Ulysse Dutoit 2003*

LEGENDA series designed by Cox Design Partnership, Witney, Oxon
Printed in Great Britain by
Information Press
Eynsham
Oxford OX8 1JJ

Chief Copy-Editor: Genevieve Hawkins

Leo Bersani, Emeritus Professor of French at the University of California at Berkeley, specializes in 19th- and 20th-century literature, psychoanalysis, literature and the visual arts, and cultural criticism.

Ulysse Dutoit, Lecturer in French at at the University of California at Berkeley, specializes in the visual arts, particularly film and painting.

Their joint publications include *The Forms of Violence* (1985), *Arts of Impoverishment: Beckett, Rothko and Resnais* (1993), *Caravaggio's Secrets* (1998) and *Caravaggio: Derek Jarman's Caravaggio* (1999). Leo Bersani is also the author of *Marcel Proust: The Fictions of Life and of Art* (1965), *Balzac to Beckett* (1970), *Baudelaire and Freud* (1979), *The Death of Stéphane Mallarmé* (1981), *The Freudian Body: Psychoanalysis and Art* (1986), *The Culture of Redemption* (1990) and *Homos* (1995).

This lecture on Godard will appear as a chapter in Leo Bersani and Ulysse Dutoit's forthcoming book, *Forms of Being/Cinema, Aesthetics, Subjectivity*, to be published by the British Film Institute.

Forming Couples: Godard's *Contempt*

Contempt cements the couple. An arguably more plausible view would be that contempt drives the couple apart, a view supported—or so it has been maintained—by Jean-Luc Godard's 1963 film *Contempt*, in which a wife's sudden contempt for her husband deals the death-blow to an idyllic intimacy. The plausibility of this view depends on a rather simple yet irreproachable psychological reading: the feeling of contempt is incompatible with the sentiment of love. It is, in this respect, different from hatred of a loved object—hatred which, as our Western experts in passionate intimacy from Racine to Freud have shown, can generally be interpreted as the disguised expression of thwarted or guilty desire. Contempt, on the other hand, would be the blocking of *any* passionate attachment; indeed, it would depend on an act of judgment that at once presupposes and enacts the extinction of passion.

Godard himself perhaps invited such a reading when, in a 1963 interview, he spoke of the subject of his film as being 'people who look at one another and judge one another, and who are then in turn looked at and judged by cinema'.[1] Looking is indeed central to *Contempt*, but the looks that express contempt as well as those that react to it, far from signifying the dissolution of the couple, reduce the entire relational field to the structure of the intimately conjoined couple. This effect can be missed only if we identify with the apparently despised husband in Godard's film. Paul, the distressed object of contempt, obsessively seeks to understand why his wife now finds him contemptible, which for him means why she has turned away from him. He thus fails to see, in a sense we will presently elaborate upon, that she has never been closer to him. And criticism makes the same mistake when, rising above Paul's anguish but remaining nonetheless faithful to his perspective, it describes *Contempt* as 'a ceremony depicting a love lost', the breakdown of 'a complete and ideal love by instances of distrust'.[2] In other words, the interpretative point of departure for criticism, as for Paul, has been the destruction of the couple. The work of interpretation then consists of looking for the cause of the estrangement, a search conducted by Paul by means of his repeated, unsuccessful demand: 'Dis-moi pourquoi tu me méprises' ('Tell me why you feel contempt for me').

We want to ask a very different question: what is the *appeal* of contempt, both for Camille and for Godard as a film-maker? This is by no means to suggest that Camille and Godard are, as it were, attracted to contempt for the same reasons. But in both cases we will be turning our attention away from the psychic origins of contempt and towards its effects in the world. In the case of Camille, this means examining the strategic advantages of contempt rather than the psychic events leading to a devastating ethical judgment. And in the case of the film-maker, the question can only be: what does contempt do to cinematic space? How does it affect the visual field with which Godard works, and especially the range and kinds of movement allowed for within that space?

Paul Javal (Michel Piccoli), a writer whose unrealized ideal is to write for the theatre, is offered a well-paid job by the brash, vulgar, macho American producer Jeremy Prokosch (Jack Palance). Prokosch is producing a film version of Homer's *Odyssey*; unhappy with the work of his director Fritz Lang (played by Fritz Lang), Prokosch wants to hire Paul 'to write some new scenes for the *Odyssey* ... not just sex ... but more ... more'.[3] The producer, as Paul immediately sees, does not really know exactly what he wants 'more' of (except for the sex), but he probably means more of the sort of Hollywood spectacle with which Lang is of course only too familiar and which he apparently refuses to provide. Paul, whose sympathies will be with Lang rather than with Jerry, is nonetheless tempted to accept the latter's offer because, as Prokosch accurately and maliciously tells him, he needs the money and has a very beautiful wife. The wife is Camille, a 28-year-old former secretary (Brigitte Bardot), and Paul needs the money to pay for an apartment they have just bought in Rome (where the first two-thirds of the film takes place). This potentially providential arrangement is endangered very early in the film when, invited by Jerry to come to his place for a drink after seeing some rushes from the *Odyssey* at Cinecittà, Paul encourages Camille to drive with Jerry in his red Alfa Romeo to the producer's home while he, Paul, will take a cab. This begins the fall from that happy period of their love when, as Camille says in a voice-over later on, 'Everything happened with a rapid, mad, enchanted spontaneity and I would find myself once again in Paul's arms without remembering what had happened.' Camille will now repeatedly look at Paul with distrust and aversion, and, at the end of the extraordinary scene in their apartment which takes up one-third of the film—a scene at once tedious, oppressive and brilliantly executed—she announces to Paul that she no longer loves him, that in fact she has only contempt for him. Camille nonetheless accompanies Paul to Capri, where part of the *Odyssey* will be filmed. Her contempt is perhaps irrevocably confirmed when Paul, repeating his earlier, presumably despicable, behaviour, encourages Camille to return with Jerry to the producer's villa while he, Paul, stays on the boat where Lang and his crew have been shooting scenes from the Nausicaa episode in Homer. While Camille will later say that she would rather die than reveal the reasons for her contempt, and while Paul's unrelenting and anguished pressure can make her say nothing more specific than the accusation: 'You're not a man', nearly all the film's spectators seem to share Paul's final speculation: Camille feels that Paul, sensing that Prokosch is attracted to her, has been encouraging her to be alone with the producer as a way of securing Jerry's professional good graces. Although Paul, hoping to convince Camille that her suspicions are unfounded, will announce his decision not to continue with the film (and to return to his writing for the theatre), Camille's contempt is unaffected by Paul's sacrifice and she accepts a ride back to Rome with Prokosch. The two are killed in a crash seconds after Jerry speeds his Alfa Romeo out of a service station onto the autostrada and into a truck. The film ends with Paul's farewell to Lang on the roof-terrace of the Villa Malaparte in Capri. Lang, who says that we must finish what we have begun, is shooting the scene of Odysseus' first view of Ithaca at the end of his ten-year voyage home from the Trojan War. Godard's and Lang's cameras approach one another by means of diagonal tracking movements from right to left; at the point where they are about to meet, Godard's camera continues its progress with a pan from right to left that leaves behind Lang and his crew (including Godard, who appears briefly as Lang's assistant) and the actor playing Odysseus who is filmed from behind, arms raised, looking over the sea towards his homeland. The final image, in which we do *not* see Ithaca, is a still of the sea and the sky; we hear the word 'Silence!' twice (once in French, the voice is Godard's, and once in Italian), and the word FIN, in blue letters against a black background, will itself disappear in a final black dissolve.

We risk the tedium of this plot summary in order to emphasize the unpromising and improbable nature of the film's 'story'. While the vast number of interviews Godard has given—and especially the more recent ones—bring an invaluable perspective to his work as a film-maker, some of his comments about *Contempt* do not take us much further than the presumed psychological or ethical lesson to be learned from this story. The film, he claimed in an interview from the same year the work came out, should give us 'a fleeting feeling of the vanity of all things'. *Contempt* is about men cut off from the gods and from the world, and the drama of Camille and Paul is that of a chance misunderstanding that somehow ends in catastrophe.[4] Such statements might describe the mediocre novel by Alberto Moravia, *Il Disprezzo*, from which the film was taken, but have nothing to say about the confrontation between that novel, which also includes the account of a filmic version of the *Odyssey*, and the Godard film which at once imitates and betrays the relation in the novel between the doomed contemporary couple and the filming of the ancient epic that celebrates the marriage of Odysseus and Penelope. Godard was aware of the poor quality of his literary source. He called Moravia's novel a common *roman de gare*—the kind of book you buy before boarding a train—'full of classical and outmoded feelings, in spite of the modernity of the situations. But', he added, 'it's with that kind of novel that beautiful films are often made.'[5]

What is the secret of this cinematic alchemy? Godard puts into question the interest and even the ethical validity of a subject treated by Moravia with great seriousness: desire and lost love. Moravia's work unintentionally parodies the literature of desire and of psychological analysis to which it belongs. While exploiting a mildly clever analogy and contrast between the desire-ridden modern couple and the (presumably) psychologically neutral couple of Homer's world, Moravia manages to make of that contrast nothing more than the melancholy and mystified longing of a psychologically saturated consciousness. Godard is also interested in the relation to Homer, especially, it would seem, in the connections between the modern couple's estrangement and Odysseus and Penelope's marriage. His film implicitly asks how the modern couple 'remembers' the ancient couple, and in so doing it proposes an original and valuable view of any presumed relation to the past. Both the film and the novel offer an interpretation of Odysseus and Penelope's marriage in which it prefigures the troubled union of Camille and Paul in Godard, and Riccardo and Emilia in Moravia. This reading is proposed by the German director Reingold in *Il Disprezzo*; it is initiated by Prokosch and stubbornly and unconvincedly elaborated by Paul in *Le Mépris*. The intellectually smug Reingold insists on modernizing *The Odyssey*, by which he means dissecting it, examining its internal mechanism, and putting it together again, as he says, 'according to our modern requirements'. These requirements are, unsurprisingly, psychological, more specifically, psychoanalytic: 'we shall', Reingold promises (or warns) Riccardo, 'explore the mind of Ulysses—or rather, his subconscious.'[6] The dissection and exploration lead to an interpretation echoed by Paul in his conversation with Lang in Capri. Reingold summarizes his findings for Riccardo:

Point one: Penelope despises Ulysses for not having reacted like a man, like a husband, and like a king, to the indiscreet behaviour of the Suitors ... Point two: her contempt causes the departure of Ulysses to the Trojan War ... Point three: Ulysses, knowing that he is awaited at home by a woman who despises him, delays his return as long as he can ... Point four: in order to regain Penelope's esteem and love, Ulysses slays the Suitors ... d'you understand, Molteni?[7]

Godard gives to Lang Riccardo's refutation of this psychologizing rewriting of *The Odyssey*, a refutation that implicitly appeals to the theory of epic objectivity developed by Hegel in the section of the *Aesthetics* devoted to poetry. Lang's argument repeats almost word for word this impassioned response on the part of Riccardo to Reingold's reading of Homer:

The beauty of the *Odyssey* consists precisely in the belief in reality as it is and as it presents itself objectively ... in this same form, in fact, which allows of no analysis or dissection and which is exactly what it is: take it or leave it ... In other words ... the world of Homer is a real world ... Homer belonged to a civilization which had developed in accordance with, not in antagonism to, nature ...That is why Homer believed in the reality of the perceptible world and saw it in a direct way, as he represented it, and that is why we too should accept it as it is, believing in it as Homer believed in it, literally, without going out of our way to look for hidden meanings.[8]

Godard obviously sympathizes with Lang, but, as we shall see, his film is also ironic about any secure view of the past; it implicitly puts into question the assumption that the past is finished and that it can therefore be known. On the other hand, in *Il Disprezzo* (which is narrated in the first person from Riccardo's point of view), nothing indicates that Moravia takes any distance either from Riccardo's view of Homer in the passage just quoted or from the extremely muddled and self-serving application of that view, at the end of the novel, to Emilia and himself. Godard, happily, simply ignores that application; it has something to do with Riccardo now belonging to an 'ideal world', to which, through his reading of Homer as belonging to the 'real world' (?), he somehow aspires. He is determined to raise Emilia to his level, Emilia who is seen at once as having the simplicity and genuineness of nature and the miserable conventionality of 'the perfectly real world of people like Battista and Reingold'.[9] Most tellingly, Moravia's sympathy with the non-psychological relationality of Homer's world has no effect on the kind of novel he writes. Riccardo's sense of impotence—his sentimentalizing distancing of the Homeric as something ideal and inaccessible, something that does not exist but to which he should nonetheless aspire—is echoed in Moravia's own inability to take any distance at all from his psychological fiction. Godard, instead of simply lamenting our imprisonment in a psychologized consciousness, will make us see both the damage done to the relational field by that consciousness *and* the possibility of a field in which relational lines might be drawn differently.

Il Disprezzo oppressively repeats, from beginning to end, Riccardo's anguished curiosity about the reasons for Emilia's contempt. It is, in other words, a novel about the impenetrability of the other's desires—just as, we might say, much of Proust's great novel is. But Moravia never asks the more interesting questions to which this curiosity might give rise, such as: what is the relation between passion itself and the loved one's turning away from the lover? can the pursuit of the other's desires avoid becoming a crisis of *self*-identification? in what sense might the estrangement of the passionate couple be said to reveal the estrangement constitutive of passionate coupling itself (thus confirming Lacan's famous dictum: 'There is no sexual relation')? We are not saying that Moravia should have asked exactly these (Proustian) questions, but we are saying that if his novel is a *roman de gare*, it is because it is never more than the story it tells, because he is never pressured by that story into a speculation on the nature of its elements, about, specifically in this case, the nature of sexual passion. Its thematic subject is all there is. *Il Disprezzo* is the hothouse preservation of the psychological novel after that novel had been dissolved, as an explorable genre, by the climactic dissections of Proust.

Any such dissection would have depended on the impenetrable Emilia being put into sharper focus. The question of *what contempt does* can only be answered if the contemptuous subject's remoteness and passivity are demystified. This is not at all the same as asking why Emilia or Camille feels contempt. Moravia does show us that Emilia's contempt immobilizes Riccardo in his passion, but nothing much can be made of that demonstration unless it expands into a critique of contempt itself. Godard has said that he had originally wanted Kim Novak for the role of Camille. Novak has, he added, 'a passive, placid character ... a soft character. Her mystery is her softness.' That is a good description of Moravia's Emilia, but a bad description of Godard's Camille, that is, of Brigitte Bardot. In the same interview Godard recognizes this when he specifies that '[Camille's] character came from what is Bardot'. Unlike Paul, 'whose psychology can be justified—on a purely psychological level', Bardot is 'a block. You have to take it as a block, all in one piece. That's why it's interesting.'[10] Bardot could not be transformed into Camille; Godard had to take her as Bardot, to let her simply be.

And how was she? There is an amusing reference to Bardot within the film when, in response to Camille's asking for the source of one of his literary quotations, Lang identifies it as 'an excerpt from a ballad by poor B.B.'. Paul asks: 'Bertold Brecht?' just as Camille, with the trace of a smile, walks out of the frame and Lang answers: 'Yes.' Camille is Bardot-ized more spectacularly, and more significantly, in the film's opening scene, the one wholly contempt-free sequence. At the insistence of Joe Levine, the film's executive producer, who apparently thought there was not enough of Bardot in the film, enough of what Bardot, at the height of her fame, was most famous for, Godard added this scene of the naked Bardot lying in bed next to Paul. The sequence immediately follows the film's credits, which are given not as a written text (except for the title: *Le Mépris*, red letters on a black background), but in voice-over. The recital of the credits is visually accompanied by a scene that, at the very beginning of the film and in a very literal way, brings the mechanics of film-making, and of film-looking, to the forefront of our attention. A Mitchell camera is shown moving towards us on tracks from the right background. The cameraman and two technicians are filming Francesca, Prokosch's assistant (Georgia Moll), as she walks towards us to the left of the tracks. When the camera arrives just in front of where it is being filmed by Godard's camera, it makes a 45-degree pan to the left so that it is facing us and then tilts downward until it and Godard's camera, which has been filming the scene from below, are directly framing each other. Godard's camera films Coutard's camera filming it. At the very beginning of *Contempt*—even 'before' *Contempt*—this sequence threatens the visual impunity we generally enjoy in looking at films. In the darkness of the movie house, we alone do the looking; the filmic images cannot look back at the spectator's protected, intact body. The title sequence of *Contempt*, by emphasizing the physicality of the filming process, paradoxically brings that process close to theatre, where the spectator, though also 'lost' and inviolate in a darkened room, must always confront real bodies who at any moment may really move towards him, as Coutard's camera moves towards us. While Coutard is of course not filming the spectator's body, his camera has captured our point of view; it is looking at the site/sight of our looking, which it has reduced to the unidentifiable circle of light we see in Coutard's lenses. And at this very moment the narrative voice perversely gives us this perhaps apocryphal quote from André Bazin as a gloss on the meaning of the film we are about to see: 'Cinema ... substitutes for our look a world in accord with our desires. *Contempt* is the story [or history: *l'histoire*] of that world.' We say 'perversely' because the passage is recited just at the moment when we can no longer delude ourselves into thinking that film—inherently a double operation of projection and reflection—will not only allow us to look at, to visually appropriate the world without being looked at ourselves, but will also accommodate the desires that inform our looking. The exhilarating prospect that knowledge of the real—already a fantastic gain—will become the recognition of a world modelled on our desires is erased by the look directed at us by a camera-subject ignorant of and indifferent to our desires.

It is, however, immediately after the (pseudo-)Bazin quote that we see the specular ideal it expresses momentarily realized. Camille, lying naked face down on their bed, asks Paul if he loves her body, more exactly all the parts of her body, beginning with her feet and ending with her facial features. Interestingly, however, she does not tell him to look directly at her body. Instead, she begins by asking him if he can see her feet and her behind in the mirror—so that what Paul responds to (except for her face) is either his memory of those parts of Camille's body not reflected in the mirror or a framed reflection of her body. The austere warning of the title sequence is undermined by Camille's removal of herself from the real space of the bed she and Paul are lying on, of the room they are in, indeed of all the unmappable space they, like all human subjects, inhabit. By placing herself, at the very start of the sequence, within the framed security of the mirror, she defines the conditions of Paul's, and our, looking at her. Godard has given Levine Bardot with a vengeance—not simply the erotically luscious Bardot, but the visual icon that drew millions of desiring gazes to her body. The iconic power is meticulously reaffirmed through all those questions (which become fairly detailed: 'What do you prefer,' Camille asks, 'my breasts or the tips of my breasts?'—to which the compliant but perhaps slightly befuddled Paul responds: 'I don't know—both [*c'est pareil*]'). This interrogation, far from putting Bardot's body into non-totalizable pieces, seems meant to guarantee that nothing will escape being desired, that Paul's final summary of his love will be, as indeed it is, all-inclusive:

> CAMILLE: 'So you love me totally!'
> PAUL: 'Yes. I love you totally, tenderly, tragically.'

This is followed by the somewhat ambiguous concluding remark from Camille: 'Moi aussi Paul.'

    The cinemascope of *Contempt* could easily have been complicit with this splendid narcissistic display: it might have given fabulous space to the fabulous body. However, even if this were the case, Lang's dismissive reference later on to cinemascope as 'not made for men, it's made for serpents, for burials' would have retroactively inserted a sinister association—with Eve and the satanic serpent of the Garden of Eden—into the scene celebrating the naked Camille's desirability. But Godard's camera does not in fact celebrate that desirability with the generous visual dimensions of the cinemascopic screen. If Camille is verbally aiming at totality, the camera is more reticent: her whole body never occupies the screen, whose immense space is partly filled by ... the head of the bed on which they are lying! The camera pans over the parts of her body, some of which are even obscured by shadows. Godard also manages partially to redirect our attention from Bardot's body to his own formal devices: the red and blue filters that impose uniformity on the colours, the slow tracking shots along Bardot's body.[11]

    The imprisoning psychic and physical space into which Camille's contempt draws Paul is prefigured by the mirror in which his enraptured gaze visually seals a total, tender and tragic love. In that mirror Camille becomes for Paul the eminently filmable image she is for us, an image no longer subject to the existential constraints—the visual discontinuities, displacements and distractions—of real space. Contempt is the psychic version of this erotic strategy. In *Caravaggio's Secrets* we used Jean Laplanche's category of the enigmatic signifier to designate a mode of address (evoked by Caravaggio's early portraits of boys with erotically provocative poses and looks) in which the relational and visual fields are reduced to a couple immobilized by seduction, fascination and paranoia. The enigmatic signifier is Laplanche's term for an adult world infiltrated with unconscious and sexual significations and messages by which the child is seduced but which the child cannot understand. The inability to decipher the other as enigmatic signifier constitutes us as sexual beings, that is, beings in whom desire or lack is central. Desire as lack is born, we argue, as the exciting pain of a certain ignorance: the failure to penetrate the sense of the other's soliciting—through touch, voice, gesture or look—of our body. The enigmatic signifier narrows and centres our look; it is the originating model of a relationality in which subject and object are separated by the distance of an imaginary secret or a special authority, a distance that only 'knowledge' might cross or eliminate.

This is the distance created by Odette in a single night in Proust's *Un amour de Swann*. Failing to appear at a party where Swann had expected her, and not to be found in the cafés and on the boulevards of a city Proust compares to 'the realm of darkness', where, 'as though among the phantoms of the dead', the panicky Swann might have been 'searching for a lost Eurydice', Odette is transformed from an object of sensual interest into an object of erotic fascination.[12] In Godard's film contempt is the means by which Camille, now an enigmatic signifier, 'promotes' Paul's desire for her to the status of a total, inescapable and permanent passion. The initiating move of this strategy takes place in a scene that is most frequently discussed in terms of *Paul*'s behaviour. We refer to the moment when, in the face of Camille's apparent astonishment and irritation, Paul encourages her to get into Prokosch's car and to drive alone with him to the producer's home. This, presumably, is the moment of 'misunderstanding'—a misunderstanding that will somehow blossom into estrangement and catastrophe. To look at the sequence of events in this manner is to make of Camille a figure much less interesting than she actually is. It reduces her to the stupid conventionalism that does seem to characterize Moravia's Emilia: this single, at least possibly innocuous, gesture on Paul's part would be enough to make her conclude that he is not a 'man' and to give birth to her implacable and irreversible sentiment of contempt. To give some plausibility to the gap between cause and effect here, we would have to engage in the aesthetically irrelevant exercise of speculating on the hidden tensions in their love before this moment—tensions that nothing in the film authorizes us to suppose. Camille (as well as the major visual and structural tensions of the film) becomes much more interesting when we note that she is far from being a passive agent in this scene. Camille does not exactly disguise her activity, but the success with which she makes everyone—in and out of the film—fail to notice it can partly be measured by the description of this scene in the scenario of *Contempt* published by the French review *L'Avant-scène*. In front of the Cinecittà studio where rushes from *The Odyssey* have just been shown, Paul introduces Camille to Jerry, who, sitting in his car, shakes her hand looking away from her. Camille is then introduced to Lang, and she, Paul and Lang speak for a moment to the right of Jerry's car, whose motor can be heard during their exchange. While Paul goes on speaking to Lang, Camille turns away from them and goes back to Jerry's car. *L'Avant-scène* tells us that she then moves along the car and goes around it—failing to mention that, looking down at the car as she does so, her fingers glide along its surfaces so that, when she reaches the other side, she will have caressed nearly all of this metallic extension of Prokosch's body. The continuously revved-up red Alpha-Romeo is presented so obviously, even so crudely, as a manifestation, a tool of Jerry's machismo—a tool that, in its final thrust forward at the end of the film, will kill both Jerry and Camille—that it hardly seems exaggerated to speak of Camille initiating a carnal contact between the two of them in the early scene.[13] Her speech, of course, suggests just the opposite—the opposite in fact of any activity at all. Her preferred responses to questions—will she come for a drink to Jerry's house? will she accompany Paul to Capri?—are: 'I don't know', 'Perhaps', and 'My husband will decide'.

The scene just discussed interests us less as a sign of an erotic attraction to Jerry than as a ritual-like enactment of Camille's power to imprison a fascinated gaze, a power that contempt consolidates. Contempt immobilizes Paul's gaze, afflicting it with a paranoid intensity: what has he done to make himself contemptible in Camille's eyes? Paul has been stolen from himself; he is now a secret in Camille's eyes. The brilliant success of contempt as an affective strategy depends on an apparent contradiction: it fixes its object's gaze on itself at the same time that it remains invisible. By manoeuvring Paul into looking at her in order to find his own contemptible image, Camille enjoys the double advantage of being the nearly exclusive object of his look and *of not being seen*. Contempt blinds the other at the very moment it intensifies his visual attention. Contempt could thus be considered, more generally, as the psychic metaphor for a body so secure in its power to dazzle the gaze of others that it can count on not being observed. It is as if Camille–Bardot knew that our transfixed look would not *see* the way she circles Prokosch's car ...

The extraordinarily narrowing effect this has on the fields of vision of both the subject and object of contempt is brilliantly rendered in a scene on the terrace-roof of Jerry's villa (the Villa Malaparte) in Capri. The first shot shows us Camille sitting on the terrace, with the sea and the sky beyond and above her. She gets up and moves left a few steps towards the centre of the terrace, stops and waves with both arms towards the right in the direction of the cliff along whose paths Paul and Lang have been walking, discussing *The Odyssey*. She takes a few steps to the right again, and, as the music that has been accompanying her movements stops, she hastens her step and walks out of the frame at the end of a 90-degree pan to the left. The camera stops for a few seconds in a long shot of the sea, the sky and, in the left half of the frame, the cliff. We then hear Paul calling 'Camille!' just before he enters from where she has just exited. He at first retraces Camille's steps on the terrace followed by the same camera movement, but in reverse, that had traced Camille's exit. (How could they have missed each other? ...) In their self-absorption, in their search for and flight from one another, they execute the only movements in the sequence, movements curiously detached from the natural setting against which they take place. In a vast context of great stillness, their preoccupied crossing of the terrace (with Paul repeating Camille's itinerary in the opposite direction) has something mechanical and incongruous. They move without seeing anything around them, and this disconnectedness has the effect of making the cliff, the sea and the sky seem almost like a painted backdrop. It is not exactly that nature becomes insignificant; indeed, when it is framed as a mere view into which these unseeing, inattentive human figures are deposited, the natural scene becomes just that, a mere scene which, however, perhaps by virtue of this violation of its presence, takes on a somewhat ominous, threatening aspect. (A similar effect is given by the splendid but deadening framed views of the sea and the cliff through the windows of the Villa Malaparte, a structure somewhat prison-like in its magnificent promontory setting.) What Lang alludes to as the neurosis of modern man (and of the modern couple), and which Jerry and Paul project onto Odysseus and Penelope, is not simply a social or psychic phenomenon. Godard positions it within the spaces of nature, suggesting that it profoundly modifies our relation to those spaces by blocking them with dissonant human presences. A blocking that is also a kind of emptying: neurotic desire—which may be a tautology—creates voids in space. The lack inherent in the desire that at once separates and cements the passionate couple is replicated by spatial breaks at those points where, as it were, their bodies tear into space. Space becomes discontinuous when it is invaded by these foreign bodies whose inner habitat has the false extensibility of a purely psychic space.

The terrace-roof of the Villa Malaparte resembles an enormous stage. And Godard films Camille's and Paul's entrances and exits as if his camera were constrained by theatrical vision, as if, like the spectators in a theatre, he could not follow them into the 'wings' into which Camille disappears and from which Paul emerges. This is only one of several references to theatre in *Contempt*, and we might explain Godard's easy moves between the theatrical and the cinematic by referring to his claim, in a 1968 interview, that there is 'no difference between the theater and movies. It is all theater.' But, as he goes on to say, 'it is simply a matter of understanding what theater means'.[14] And theatre means differently in film and on the stage. 'It is all theater' may be nothing more than a way of reminding us that while theatre can do without film, film cannot do without theatre. In film, only the most thoroughly discontinuous and unrealistic (or surrealist) succession of images might succeed in being wholly inhospitable to presentation on a stage. There are, however, major differences. Not only is our relation to bodies as images necessarily different from our relation to real bodies present at the time we are seeing them; the filmic medium may also be intrinsically uncongenial to certain major forms of theatrical drama. While films, for example, can of course imitate theatrical time and thereby submit to the temporal irreversibility necessary for tragedy, film also makes possible a very different, non-tragic time. The time of tragic drama is inexorably narrativized time; temporal sequence in film, on the other hand, is the result of a decision. It is, more precisely, an effect of montage, which may make it difficult for someone like Godard, who has spoken of montage as the defining feature of film as an art form, to take seriously the *necessity* inherent in tragedy. *Contempt*, which Godard characterized as 'un peu hollywoodien', is his most classical, realistic film, and it thereby seems to obey the narrative rule of temporal irreversibility. But, interestingly, Camille's and Jerry's deaths are not the film's climax; it ends, instead, with the shooting of a scene from Lang's film followed by a shot that (we will return to this) is outside both the narrative of *Contempt* and the narrative of *The Odyssey*. And yet something we might call the tragic is central to *Contempt*, although it should not be defined in either affective or ethical terms. Rather it has something to do with the human disconnecting itself from the space it inhabits. The loss or the violation of space is the loss of the filmic itself. The tragedy of the modern couple's claustrophobic self-absorption is its destructive effect on what surrounds them—or, more exactly, on the film-maker's ability to compose a relatedness between the human and the non-human. Camille and Paul sin against the cinemascopic; to film them, perhaps only the close-up would be entirely appropriate.

And yet the close-up is an ambiguous means of characterization, or even of identification. In *Arts of Impoverishment* we discuss the last sequence of Alain Resnais's *Mon Oncle d'Amérique* as a powerful illustration of the *dis-* or *mis*-identifying effects of visual *rapprochement*. The film ends with eight still shots of a brick wall, a wall on which a forest has been painted. Each shot, in abrupt and discontinuous transition from one fixed angle of vision to the next, brings us closer to the wall while thrusting upon us the ambiguity of the object being approached. The closer we get to the wall, the less we see. Not only is the narrowing of the field of vision made disorienting by the spaces on the wall that are skipped from one still to the next; it also becomes more and more difficult to describe the wall itself. We are shifted from a subject (a building with a scene from nature painted on it) to elements of construction. We recognize a building, but then the camera focuses on a giant tree, then on tree trunks, and finally to spots of paint on the bricks. We become more and more conscious of the bricks through the forest, and the trees finally disappear into the building, the human edifice, which is their only reality. And yet the final shot of a single brick brings us back to the earth from which the entire building has been made. The wall's identity is unlocatably somewhere between nature and artifice: it is nature composed, constructed, a nature we see representing itself *as* nature.[15]

Even more radical effects can be obtained when the camera approaches a human face. Speaking of the mysterious resemblance between the two women's faces in Bergman's *Persona*, Gilles Deleuze writes that the close-up has pushed the face 'into those regions where the principle of individuation no longer holds sway'. Bergman simultaneously films the face and its erasure, 'the fear of the face confronting its own nothingness'. *Contempt* stops short of filming what Deleuze calls 'the nihilism of the face',[16] but the close-ups of Camille and Paul are either psychologically inexpressive or psychologically impenetrable. If we read 'contempt' into the close-ups of Camille's face, it is because the film's title and Camille herself (when she reveals her contempt to Paul) have identified the film's apparent subject for us. In fact, there are shots of her—perhaps especially when she looks fixedly and silently at Paul in the garden of Jerry's home in Rome—in which she resembles the statues of the gods from Lang's *Odyssey*: still, immobile and impenetrable. To say that these looks express contempt, or a mixture of aversion, astonishment and distress (as well as a silent and desperate appeal to Paul), is to speculate, as Paul is forced to do, on what the enigmatic signifier is concealing. Even with Paul, the close-up can be psychologically mystifying. Having settled into a chair on the boat from which scenes for *The Odyssey* are being filmed, and having encouraged Camille to return to the villa with Jerry, Paul lights a cigarette as the camera moves in for a close-up. Piccoli brilliantly plays this moment as an opportunity for an expressiveness at once inviting and resisting interpretation. Something flaccid, passive, 'unmanly' as Camille might call it, seems to tell a pathetic story not exactly of his pushing his wife into Jerry's arms, but simply of a certain relief at being free of her for the moment so he can enjoy watching the naked actresses diving into the water. Or perhaps what he is showing is his weariness with Camille's inability to move beyond him, to circulate less obsessively, less passionately, in the world. He tells her here, as he did in the car sequence at Cinecittà: 'Vas-y! Vas-y!' ('Go ahead!'), an exhortation repeated several times and which may be his clumsy way of initiating other movements, other directions for both of them.

But the only certain thing about all such speculations is that they remove us from the film. All this is in our heads, not on the screen; the characters' motivations, unarticulated by them and invented by us, are a substitute for our only legitimate activity: the activity of looking and of registering what we *see*. To explore Camille's and even Paul's psychology is to play the game of the enigmatic signifier, that is, to be complicit with the anti-cinematic visuality it embodies. With our interpretations we emphasize how expressive their faces are, but expressiveness is perhaps always an exaggeration of expression, the cue for a reading there will be no reason to stop. To interpret the expressive face is to abandon the face that belongs to a visible body. Godard will, so to speak, defend himself against the threat to his visual space inherent in the very subject he has chosen for the visual space called *Contempt*. What would non-expressive objects be like? Can a film be sufficiently lighted, can a film-maker get the light right (an obsessive concern in Godard's 1981 masterpiece *Passion*) without the 'extra lighting' of the expressive? In answering these questions Godard will have saved his film from being absorbed into, and victimized by, its psychic drama.

Might there be another type of couple? Might Penelope and Odysseus be the model for a different sort of intimacy? Psychological interpretations of the ancient couple are discredited from the start by virtue of the fact that it is Prokosch who first proposes one. His theory about *The Odyssey* is that 'Penelope has been unfaithful'. When Paul tells Camille in Capri that he defends Prokosch's theory, he reformulates it with a somewhat different emphasis. '*The Odyssey* is the story of a man who loves his wife, who doesn't love him.' Earlier, in the movie theatre in Rome, he had proposed yet another interpretation. Odysseus went off to Troy because he was sick of Penelope, and because of that he made his return voyage last as long as possible. Lang mockingly asks Camille, who is sitting next to him in this scene, if she thinks that is Paul's idea or Jerry's. Similarly, Camille's only answer to Paul's assertion that Penelope did not love Odysseus is: 'I'm sure you don't really think that.' These various interpretative stabs come together in the more coherent if no more persuasive account Paul gives to Lang during their walk back to the villa in Capri. Now Odysseus' reluctance to return home is the result of an estrangement very much like Paul and Camille's. Odysseus had encouraged Penelope to be nice (*aimable*) to the suitors, to let them court her and to accept their gifts. Not taking the suitors seriously as rivals, he preferred not to risk the scandal of throwing them out. But this conduct leads Penelope, 'a fundamentally simple woman', to feel contempt for Odysseus and to stop loving him. Poor Odysseus, realizing too late that 'his excessive prudence' had made him lose his wife's love, concludes that the only way to win back her love is to murder the suitors.

Homeric criticism, we might say in passing, has not been entirely free of psychological interpretations of *The Odyssey*. Telemachus' 'harshness' towards his mother, his 'brusquely ungracious' manner of addressing her, have given rise to the suggestion that he suspects his mother of secretly wishing to marry one of the suitors. There has also been speculation about his own difficulties in growing to manhood 'without the correction and support of a father'. Might we not also speak of 'impulses that lurk dormant below the surface of Penelope's conscious mind', impulses prompted but not created by Athena when the goddess inspires her with a longing 'to display herself to her suitors, fan their heart, / inflame them more'?[17] Homer's work does not exactly contradict such conjectures, but it is also far from hospitable to them. While specific passages might appear to authorize assumptions of psychic depth, the entire epic is indifferent to them. The text of *The Odyssey* is not a psychological world. It is not the world of Euripides, and the universe in which Telemachus moves is not one that can even recognize, much less be modified by, a Hamlet-like brooding about a mother's betrayal. *The Odyssey* is the fabulous Captain Marvel comics or, closer to us, the Aegean Star Wars (the Wave Wars) of Antiquity. It is above all Odysseus' wonderfully improbable adventures in the wonderfully improbable geography of his voyage. The obstacles to his returning home are the *raison d'être* of the story about his returning home. They provide the adventures of the epic, the encounters with figures and events unconstrained by the limits of realistic representation. The gods are not (or are not primarily) metaphors for human passions in Homer (as they are, say, in Euripides' *Hippolytus*); their magical powers are their most important attribute, their major contribution to Odysseus' adventures. *The Odyssey* is above all Circe, the one-eyed, man-eating giant Cyclops, the Kingdom of the Dead, the sirens, Scylla and Charybdis, the cattle of the Sun .... The appetite for fabulous stories is itself so fabulous, so excessive, that the tales of Odysseus' wanderings include not only his 'real' adventures on the Aegean Sea and in continental Greece, but also the false ones he invents disguised as a beggar on his return to Ithaca, adventures that extend his travels to Crete, Cyprus, Phoenicia and Sicily. Indeed, the actual travelling seems less important than the stories to which it gives rise: Odysseus and Telemachus willingly suspend their own projects in order to listen to tales told by their hosts. If, as Paul in *Contempt* suggests, Odysseus really doesn't want to return home, it is not because of any complicated feelings about Penelope, but rather because not returning home *is The Odyssey*. Odysseus' marriage and his desire to be again with Penelope are what Henry James would have called the compositional convenience that allows what interests Homer, and us, to take place. Bereft of any significance—and especially of any psychological significance—Odysseus and Penelope as a couple provide the useful, and empty, narrative pretext thanks to which Odysseus can wander alone.

We can, then, easily agree with Lang's objection to Paul that Odysseus 'is not a modern neurotic, he was a simple, wily and fearless man'. But the relation of Lang's view of Homer's world as 'a real world' that has to be taken exactly as it is, and of *The Odyssey* as dramatizing the struggle of individuals against circumstances and against the gods, to either the ancient epic or to Lang's own filmed version of it is much less clear. The few shots we see from Lang's film certainly have nothing to do with either the content or the intellectual solemnity of his theories. The gods are painted plaster statues; there are a few shots of the actor playing Odysseus, one profile shot of a heavily made-up, very young Penelope. The only action shot is of Odysseus stretching his bow and shooting an arrow that we then see implanted in another bearded man's neck, from which a stream of very red blood is flowing. The statue of Poseidon, Odysseus' enemy, returns at certain moments in the film, accompanied by Georges Delerue's dramatic music, as a kind of ominous visual mark of the doom towards which Paul and Camille's relation is inexorably moving. It is as if neither Lang nor Godard were interested in documenting their resistance to the psychologizing of *The Odyssey*, in giving us at least some idea of what a presumably faithful rendering of Homer might look like. What does seem to interest Godard is the possibility of a *non-interpretative* way of relating to *The Odyssey*. In *Contempt*, this means subordinating the 'truth' about *The Odyssey* to an interest in the kind of relations we can have to it. Not what *The Odyssey* is about, but the sort of relation we establish with it when we ask what it is about. To ask about this is one way of exploring our possible modes of connecting to the past. The mode most familiar to us is one of epistemological appropriation. Even when we acknowledge the immense difficulty of knowing the past, we are always doing our best. Should we study great events and great leaders, or the ordinary lives of ordinary people? Whatever alternatives we struggle with, whatever arguments we engage in, the assumption is always that some degree of knowledge might be possible, that the (perhaps impossible) ideal would be 'to get things right'. In other words, questions of knowledge nearly always take precedence over questions about what the past is, about the nature of its pastness. *Contempt* brilliantly reverses this priority of epistemology over ontology.

Crucial to this reversal is what we referred to a moment ago as the film's non-interpretative relation to *The Odyssey*. In the place of an interest in the truth about either the modern couple or the ancient couple, Godard redirects our attentions to the coupling itself—not to the coupling between Camille and Paul, or between Penelope and Odysseus, but to the coupling between the two couples. This has enormous consequences for the view of time in the film (as well as of filmic time), but we might first of all note that the relation between the modern and the ancient couple in *Contempt* is but one of several alternative couplings in the film. In a 1975 interview for *Le Monde* Godard spoke of the couple in his film *Numéro deux* as living 'in symbiosis with other couples that are just as fundamental: parents–children, kids–grown-ups, young women–old women, factory–house'.[18] In *Contempt* Godard is complicitous with the destruction of Paul and Camille as a couple, not because he sees more profoundly than they do both the psychic climate and the chance events that make their separation inevitable, but rather because he has so many other views of how people and things might come together. There is, first of all and most simply, the possibility of Camille being moved from her relation to Paul to a relation with Prokosch. Even this, however, is not exactly psychically motivated: nothing (except that tactile circling of his car ...) suggests that she desires Prokosch or is even very interested in him. Rather, they are visually paired in ways that suggest some sort of immediate physical bond as well as a more mysterious bond of which they are certainly unaware. We see the spontaneous physical bond in their walking side by side in step towards Paul outside Jerry's home in Rome, and especially in the two scenes of their speeding out of the frame in Jerry's car, once in Rome and, at the end, out of the service-station into a truck. Their possible coupling is from the first associated with the car, the instrument of their death. There is, finally, the image of their moving away together in the small boat that takes them back to the Villa Malaparte. This scene ends with a shot of the sea as their boat disappears into the horizon, leaving a trace of water in its wake, a shot almost exactly duplicated, except for the sign of the boat's passage, in the last image of the film. They are, then, coupled—inexactly coupled—to that which seems most alien to them: nature without people, without place, without circumstance. This last coupling is, at most, suggestive; it tells us nothing 'about' Camille and Jerry, it is simply another variation, something tried out, something that adds to the difficulty of saying where or what the couple is. There is also the statue in Paul and Camille's apartment, a silent, immobile, inanimate presence that, throughout this extended sequence of imprisoning estrangement, provides other, shifting modes of contiguity. At times the statue, positioned between Paul and Camille, de-couples them, at other times it couples with one or the other human partner: with Paul when he knocks on its surface (remarking that it doesn't make the same sound all over), with Camille when, for example, standing with her head bent slightly forward, she briefly appears as a formal doubling of the statue.

A kind of doubling *manqué* is central to *Contempt*'s structure. *Contempt* the film is an inaccurate rendering of Moravia's *Il Disprezzo*. The relation between Paul and Camille may or may not be a faithful rendering of the hidden sense of the relation between Odysseus and Penelope. Lang's film and Homer's epic form yet another couple, but it is impossible to say what kind of fit there is between them. And Godard's film at times films Lang's film, but it of course includes more than what it incorporates of Lang's film. Film in *Contempt* moves in and out of an uneasy aesthetic coupling with theatre. They are in certain respects complementary partners; from other perspectives— reversible vs. irreversible time, real bodies vs. images of bodies, real space vs. scenery space—they are aesthetic opposites. Pairing is thus shown to have centrifugal as well as centripetal energies. In the intimately conjoined couple, self-extension serves principally to reduce the desired other to a reflection of the desiring subject. Paul's love gives a seal of desirability to the images of herself Camille sees in the mirror; Camille's contempt condemns Paul to an unending search in her for the contemptible subject he has become. The lure of specularity is undoubtedly also present in centrifugal coupling, but it can be defeated by the pleasures of inaccurate replications. The bad fit adds to both self-identificatory and complementary coupling a type of coupling compatible with heterogeneity—and heterogeneity in this mode of coupling is a non-threatening, perhaps indistinguishable supplement to a specularity it defeats by adhering to it.

The alternative coupling proposed by *Contempt* could also be defined as translation. One of the most striking aspects of the film is its linguistic heterogeneity. Several languages are spoken: French, English and, to a lesser extent, German and Italian. And they are not merely spoken: considerable time is taken to translate Jerry's English into French, Paul and Camille's French into English, Lang's German quotations (one from Hölderlin, one that is a German translation from Dante's Italian) into French, and, somewhat superfluously, the Italian directions on the set into French (*Silenzio* to *Silence* [!]). Lang compliments Francesca, who does nearly all the translating in the film, for her French rendering of the verses from Hölderlin, but her translations of Jerry's, or Lang's, English are at times conspicuously casual, or even off. When Jerry, delighted at the rushes of a nude mermaid, says: 'Fritz, that's wonderful for you and me, but do you think the public is gonna understand that?', Francesca translates: 'C'est de l'art, mais est-ce que le public comprendra?' At one point her translation comes before what it is meant to translate: 'Toutes les émotions humaines' precedes Jerry's 'All the real human emotions'. Finally, *Contempt* uses the Latin names for the Greek gods: Homer's Poseidon is referred to as Neptune, Athena becomes Minerva.

Translation is a coupling in time. Ordinarily, an original text or speech precedes the translated version of it. As its etymology indicates, translation is a carrying over, the moving of a text from one linguistic 'place' to another. It is also, as it has often been said, a betrayal: the relation between the translation and the original can never be an identity. More interesting, however, and more difficult to determine, is the mode in which the original persists, or lasts, into the translation. The idea of betrayal, after all, includes a questionable assumption: there is, or there was, an original that could be betrayed, and that remains, somewhere, as a past event. We are not arguing, absurdly, that Dante's *Divine Comedy* and Hölderlin's poetry do not exist as texts than can be read in Italian or German. We do want to suggest that, *within the translation*, there is a relation that is neither a betrayal nor an identity nor, finally, a coming after or a coming before. And this relation, which is a kind of temporality without priority, can be a model for the passionate couple's necessary (in our view) dissolution. Let us think of translation as the *opening* of the text to be translated, its removal from a supposed textual finality and its renewal as something still in the process of being made. In translations—but also in quotations, as well as in criticism—texts enter time, a time in which they can be diversely repeated without ever being wholly realized. Godard quotes inordinately in his films—through passages projected onto the screen, or through characters who recite bits of literary texts, or directly from books. Pierre Bourdieu apparently told Godard that his candidacy to the Collège de France, which Bourdieu supported, would be rejected because Godard was thought to be insufficiently literary. This is a peculiar judgment of someone we could easily think of as the most literary of film-makers. But Godard himself has spoken of 'my royal enemy, my number one enemy, the text', and he also said: 'For me, texts are death, images are life'.[19] The professors at the Collège saw something important (which should have made them embrace Godard instead of rejecting him ...): he destroys the text as monument. By citationally picking at literature, he demonumentalizes it, therefore resurrecting it from the death of finished being, and allows it to circulate—unfinished, always being made—within the open time of film. Thanks to montage, this cinematic time can be reordered; 'physically,' Godard has said, 'you have a moment, like an object, like this ashtray. You have the present, past and future.'[20] The present, past and future as indefinite, as never having finally taken place, and never being destined to take place. In film, time's 'places' are light; they can be shifted. Film is the aesthetic medium that allows us to see the openness, the always-taking-place, which is the incorporative mode of translation and citation.

The Deleuzian and, by way of Deleuze, Bergsonian accent of their remarks should be clear. In his important work on cinema Deleuze has defined 'the profound Bergsonism of cinema in general' as 'the open totality and the event in the course of happening'.[21] In its alternative pairings *Contempt* proposes a non-copulative mode of pairing. With its centrifugal doublings, its use of translation and citation, its implicit reflexiveness on the nature of film, Godard's work proposes various models for a relocating of the partners in the passionate couple. We referred earlier to a critical reshifting of relational terms: from Paul and Camille as a couple, and Odysseus and Penelope as a couple, to the pairing of the two couples. Thematically, a naïve question is asked in the film: what are the similarities or differences between the modern and the ancient couples? This question is, so to speak, surrounded by invitations to reformulate it in terms provided by the alternative pairings we have just looked at. The question then becomes: what kind of presence do Odysseus and Penelope—and *The Odyssey*—have in the relation between Paul and Camille—and in Godard's *Contempt*? The answer has nothing to do with likeness or unlikeness, but rather with the identical ontological status of both couples: that of possibility. The past, like the present, is always *waiting to be*. Both belong, as Deleuze writes in his discussion of Bergson, to a duration 'immanent to the whole universe'. Immanent and not imminent: neither one is about to be, both constitute a universal temporal montage in which everything, always open, communicates with everything as a phenomenon of mind or spirit.[22] History is a limitlessly extensive immanence, and this affects particular bodies (like those of Paul and Camille) as an inescapable mnemonic contiguity with other bodies (such as those of Odysseus and Penelope). They have the possibility of 'remembering' other couples in history as contemporary with them—contemporary not because of some psychic or moral congeniality, but because both are unaccomplished events.[23]

But events can of course also be accomplished, in which case they become immobilized in the subject's illusion of their uniqueness. No longer *in communication*, the modern couple—a Paul and a Camille—become imprisoned in bodies that have lost the power both to remember and to see, become fixed in the false kind of memory that looks back at an infinitely remote, impenetrable and improbably similar other couple. It is as if the unending extensibility of simple duration could, at points, settle into the realized, incarnated event. No longer circulating in an always unfinished expressiveness, the events of time have become fully expressed sediments of duration, blocks of self-contained matter. This ontological fall, or sin, is also profoundly anti-aesthetic. In their sightless gravity Paul and Camille have lost the levity of imaginary being. In art, events *appear* to one another; words, images and sounds communicate indeterminately with one another, composing forms and structures only to play with the possibility of undoing forms and structures. Only the non-aesthetic is formally fixed and readable; a sign of the aesthetic is formal irresolution. Godard's film explicitly links the psychology of contempt to ethical issues: Paul's despair at no longer possessing Camille could lead him to a crime of passion; Camille would deprive Paul of his freedom by becoming, through the mystifying activity of her contempt, the only object of his look. But the ethical is shown to be inseparable from the aesthetic: the psychology of contempt is a crime against the communication and circulation of images in filmic montage. It would reduce appearances to being, duration to narrativizable history. To aestheticize our relation to the past is not to remove ourselves irresponsibly from it, but rather to live in proximity to it. It is to remind ourselves of our responsibility *not to be*. The passionately conjoined couple violate both the space they inhabit and each other. The world of *The Odyssey* is not, as it is for Moravia's Riccardo, a world to which we can, with comfortable hopelessness, aspire; it is a world whose permanently deferred sense we can't help but carry within us. Camille and Paul would have nothing to learn from Penelope and Odysseus, who remain, who must remain, non-interpretable; what Godard's couple might have done is to allow themselves to be seduced into the openness of the imaginary. By potentializing their relation *while they are in it*, they would have left their condemned coupledom and given to each other the freedom to reappear, always, as subjects too inconclusive, too multiple, too unfinished, ever to be totally loved.

This would define a new relation to space, and especially to the spaces of nature. The relation of the human to nature is undoubtedly the most important pairing—at once mysterious and utterly simple—in *Contempt*. How would nature appear if it were uninjured by what Lang refers to as human neurosis and which seems to be defined, if not by the film-maker Lang certainly by the film-maker Godard, as the inability to see? The final shot of *Contempt* seems to answer this question by presenting nature as pure appearance. When Godard's camera, having intersected with Lang's camera, leaves it and pans to the left of the actor playing Odysseus looking towards his homeland, Godard also leaves both *The Odyssey* and his own film. Lang has defined this sequence as the Homeric hero at last seeing Ithaca, but in *Contempt*'s final still shot there is no trace of a land that might be identified. The removal from this image of the human movements and agitations in both Godard's film and Homer's epic is emphasized by its differential replay of the earlier image of Camille and Jerry returning to the Villa Malaparte in a small boat we see speeding towards and disappearing into the horizon. Even with their disappearance the water's foam continues to carry traces of their passage. Any such trace of a human passage is absent from the final image. All subjects—human and narrative—are left behind. Nearly everything that would allow us to measure and to distinguish is gone. The horizon line separating sea from sky is much less sharply delineated than in the Capri shot; we have nothing—which is almost everything—but the nearly uniform spectacle of blue water and sky. Just before he climbs the huge staircase leading to the roof-terrace where Lang is shooting Odysseus' approach to Ithaca, Paul passes three large light reflectors on the lower level. It is as if Godard were suggesting that for the image we are about to see the reflectors, used to heighten light, were no longer necessary. When subjects and objects are eliminated, the exaggerations of expressiveness lose their seductive appeal. Now everything is illuminated—not with a light projected artificially onto the scene, but rather by a light from within the elements, a light that comes towards us. We too, Godard's film perhaps ultimately suggests, might also emit light, a light hidden behind psychic darkness, blocked by our expressive being. To lose our fascinating and crippling expressiveness might be the pre-condition for our moving within nature, moving as appearances registering, and responding to the call of, other appearances. No longer darkened by the demand for love, we might be ready to receive something like the splendour, the 'dazzling radiance', that Homer's 'blazing-eyed Athena' casts on the humans she protects. Bypassing his contemporary literary source, Godard may have found in Homer the ethical and aesthetic solution of a perennial problem for film-makers. To be the light may be the only certain way to get the light right.

Notes

1. *Cahiers du cinéma*, no. 46 (Aug. 1963), quoted in *Jean-Luc Godard par Jean-Luc Godard*, ed. Alain Bergala, 2 vols. (Paris: Cahiers du cinéma–Editions de l'étoile, 1985, 1998), i. 249. All translations are our own.
2. Toby Mussmann, 'Notes on *Contempt*', in his (ed.), *Jean-Luc Godard* (New York: Dutton, 1968), 146. In their excellent book on Godard, and within a much more sophisticated critical apparatus, Kaja Silverman and Harun Farocki speak of the film as a demonstration of how the 'definitive' can emerge from 'chance', of the cultural and more specifically textual conditions under which a contingent misunderstanding between Paul and Camille becomes an absolute estrangement: *Speaking about Godard* (New York: New York University Press, 1998), 42, 46–7.
3. When quoting dialogue from *Contempt*, we have consulted, and translated, the shot-by-shot analysis of the film published in *L'Avant-scène cinéma*, nos. 412–13 (May–June 1992).
4. Interview with Jean Collet, 12 Sept. 1963, quoted in *L'Avant-scène cinéma*, p. 96.
5. *Cahiers du cinéma*, no. 46 (Aug. 1963), quoted in *Godard par Godard*, i. 248.
6. Alberto Moravia, *Contempt*, trans. Angus Davidson (London: Prion, 1999), 139, 142.
7. Ibid. 190.
8. Ibid. 146.
9. Ibid. 234–5.
10. Interview with Jean Collet, 12 Sept. 1963, quoted in Mussman (ed.), *Jean-Luc Godard*, 146.
11. Another example of this disjunction between Godard's filming technique and the subject absorbing his characters can be found at the end of the apartment sequence, when Paul and Camille are seated at opposite ends of a small table, with a lamp between them. The camera moves several times during their brief dialogue from one to the other and back. But it seems curiously indifferent to their speech. When Paul begins the dialogue, he is off screen; the focus is on the lamp. The camera will begin a new tracking movement away from one of them while he or she is still speaking or is just about to speak; it will at times focus on Paul while Camille speaks and on her during his speech. The camera also has its own rhythm: a slow tracking movement followed by a more rapid one towards the end of the exchange. It is as if Godard, in being somewhat inattentive to the content of his characters' talk, were redirecting our attention both to the rhythm of his camera's movements and to linguistic rhythms rather than linguistic sense. Finally, the use of these brief tracking movements to film a scene that might have been shot from a fixed angle encompassing both Paul and Camille, or as alternating close-ups in visual accord with each one's turn at speaking, ironically emphasizes the claustrophobic nature of the entire sequence. There is movement, but it is limited, curiously mechanical in its repetitions and out of sync with the speech being recorded—as if this were the most appropriate way for the camera both to register, and to register its own distance from, the imprisoning psychic and physical space in which Camille and Paul are now moving.
12. Marcel Proust, *Swann's Way*, trans. C. K. Scott Moncrieff and Terence Kilmartin (New York: Vintage Books, 1989), 252.
13. Is Camille also enclosing Jerry within a magical circle in which, having turned

away from her when she at first offered her hand, he will from now on be unable to stop looking at her—in a manner not wholly unconnected to Penelope's (perhaps) unintentional detaining and erotic irritation of her suitors during the years of her waiting for Odysseus' return?

14. From a panel discussion at UCLA, 26 Feb. 1968; quoted in *Jean-Luc Godard: Interviews*, ed. David Sterritt (Jackson: University Press of Mississippi, 1998), 14.
15. See Leo Bersani and Ulysse Dutoit, *Arts of Impoverishment: Beckett, Rothko, Resnais* (Cambridge, MA: Harvard University Press, 1993), 173–5.
16. Gilles Deleuze, *Cinema 1: The Movement-Image*, trans. Hugh Tomlinson and Barbara Habberjam (Minneapolis: University of Minnesota Press, 1986), 100.
17. Bernard Knox, Introduction to Homer, *The Odyssey*, trans. Robert Fagles (New York: Penguin, 1996), 52–4; and *The Odyssey*, Bk 18, ll. 183–4.
18. *Godard par Godard*, i. 385.
19. The latter remark, it is true, was somewhat qualified by: 'We need both: I'm not against death': 'Alfred Hitchcock est mort,' interview in *Libération*, 2 May 1980; quoted in *Godard par Godard*, i. 416. For the former quote, see 'La curiosité du sujet', *Art Press*, special issue no. 4 (Godard) (1984–5), 5.
20. Lecture at the FEMIS, 26 Apr. 1989, in *Godard par Godard*, ii. 242.
21. Deleuze, *Cinema 1*, 206.
22. Ibid. 17.
23. 'They had the impression', we hear in voice-over as Elena and Lennox leave their home at the end of *New Wave* (1990), 'of having already lived all that. And their words seemed to become immobilized in the traces of other words from another time ... They felt tall, with above them the past, the present like identical waves of the same ocean.'